Maria de Fatima Campos was born in Brazil. She is a photographer specialising in portraiture and alternative printing processes. In 1995 she was elected Associate of the Royal Photographic Society. *Victoria's Day* was written for her daughter, Victoria, who has Down's syndrome. The book aims to show the similarities between Victoria's pre-school experiences and those of her classmates. Maria has also written *B is for Brazil, Cassio's Day: From Dawn to Dusk in a Brazilian Village*, and *Victoria Goes to Brazil* for Frances Lincoln Children's Books. She lives with her family in London.

D0281697

To the Divine Creation for trusting me to take care of Victoria.

**To all the children who contributed by appearing in this book.
Without them it wouldn't be possible.
Wishing all of them a bright and secure future.**

AUTHOR ACKNOWLEDGEMENTS
With thanks to the nursery staff team; Miss McQuillan, Ms Stow, Betty, Sandra and Debby;
to Mrs Print, reception teacher, who encouraged Victoria's independence, confidence and self-esteem;
to Wendy Armah, Victoria's learning support teacher; to Mrs Witham, the Head Teacher;
to Mrs Linda Young and Demetria, Victoria's ballet teachers; to my mother-in-law for loving Victoria and being supportive;
to my husband, Richard Davis and all the parents who agreed to co-operate in this project.
Special thanks to Janetta Otter-Barry for asking me to create a book about Victoria.

First published in Great Britain and in the USA in 2007 by
Frances Lincoln Children's Books, 74-77 White Lion Street, London N1 9PF
www.franceslincoln.com

This edition first published in Great Britain and in the USA in 2015.

A CIP catalogue record for this book is available from the British Library.

ISBN 978-1-84780-424-2

Printed in China

1 3 5 7 9 8 6 4 2

Maria de Fatima Campos

Victoria's Day

F

FRANCES LINCOLN
CHILDREN'S BOOKS

Victoria is four years old.
She lives with Mummy
and Daddy.

On a school day, Victoria gets up
at seven o'clock. Her mother combs her hair
and ties it with a red hair band.

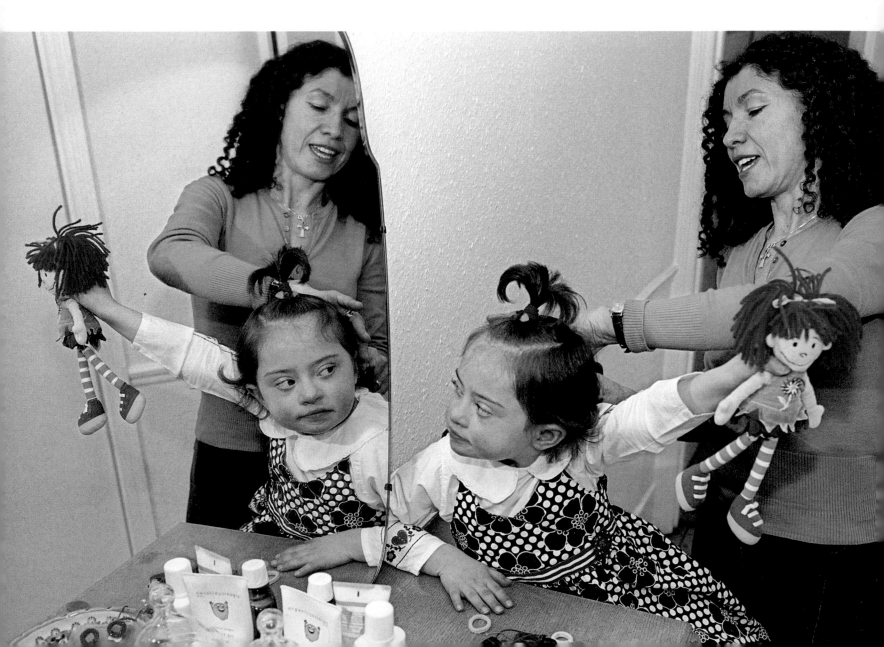

For breakfast, Victoria has berries and grated nuts with her cereal and she has hot chocolate to drink.

After breakfast Victoria brushes her teeth so her mouth feels nice and clean.

Victoria lives very close to her school. She is walking there today.

When she arrives at school Victoria hangs up her coat on her own hook.

This morning, the teacher is showing the children how to make cookies. Victoria is painting her pastry red, blue and green. Eloise is painting hers yellow. After that the pastry will be baked in the oven.

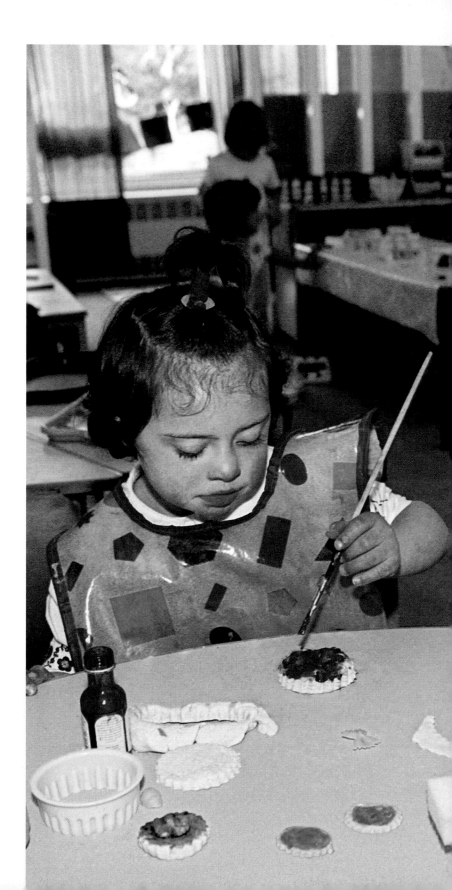

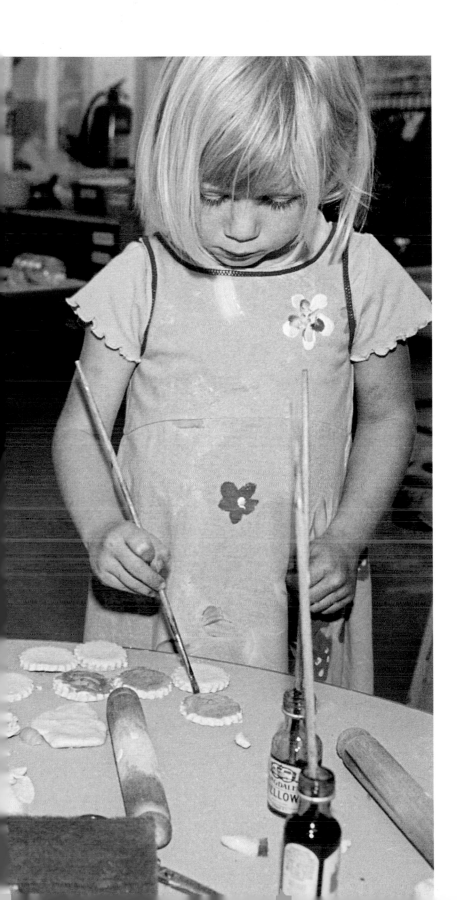

Victoria washes and
dries her hands
when she has finished.

It is playtime and everybody is going out to play. Victoria goes on the climbing-frame with her friends.

Then she joins in the tricycle ride.

Jasper is pedalling
and Max is pushing.

Victoria is feeling
thirsty so she goes
inside to have
some milk.

After playtime, Victoria, Imogen and Bianca play 'shops'. Victoria likes to count the money.

Then Victoria plays
a computer game
with Natasha.

Victoria wants to be an artist. She is painting a beautiful picture on the easel.

Ava, Tom and Max want
Victoria to play in the sand
tray with them.

The children
like pouring
out the sand
and digging
with spades.

It is time to clean up.
The children put away
all the toys.
Victoria uses a dustpan
and brush to sweep the floor.

Before hometime, the children
play games with their teacher.

Today they are pretending
to be different kinds of animals
and they make animal noises.

Then Victoria shares a book
with Max while she waits
for Mummy to pick her up.

In the afternoon, Victoria has a ballet lesson.
The children follow the sound of the piano
and try to dance on their toes. It is very hard!

After ballet, Daddy takes Victoria to the park.

She likes to feed the ducks and geese.

On the way home, Victoria goes to the farmers' market with Daddy. She loves shopping and choosing things to eat.

Victoria loves
helping Mummy
do the cooking.
Today Victoria is
peeling the carrots
while Mummy
peels the potatoes
to be cooked
for dinner.

Victoria has a bath every day after dinner. She loves to play with the bubbles and her toys in the bath. Then Mummy helps Victoria put on her pyjamas, brush her teeth and get ready for bed.

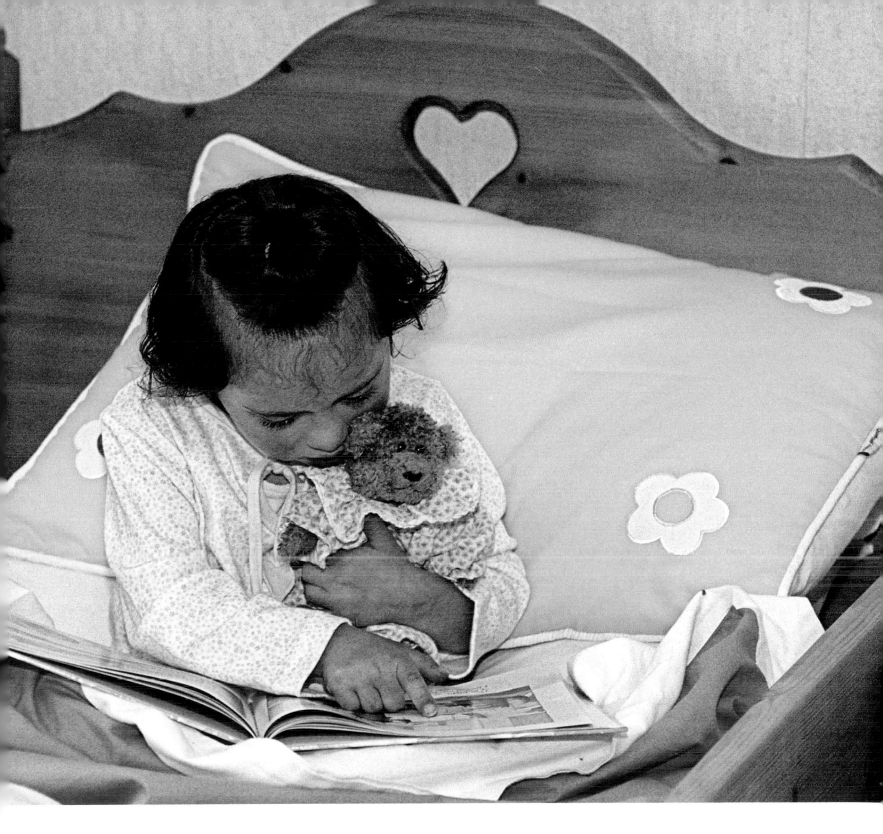

When she gets into bed, Victoria reads a new story to Teddy.

But she only goes to sleep after Mummy reads
her a story, gives her a cuddle and lots of kisses.

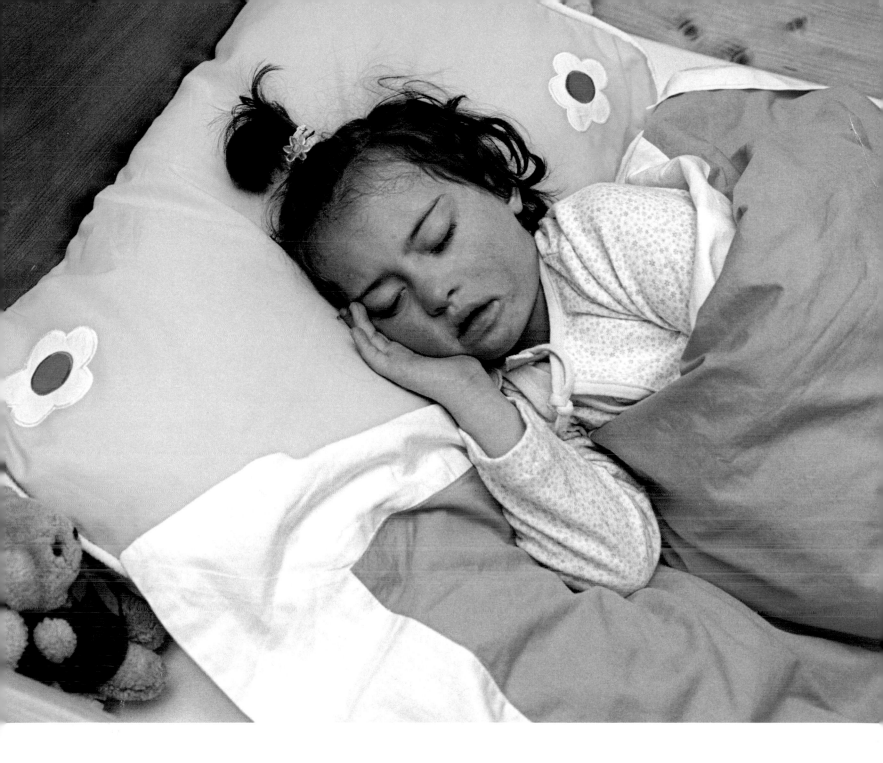

Good night, Victoria.

Victoria was born with Down's syndrome, a genetic condition caused by a baby being born with three copies of chromosome 21 instead of two. People with Down's syndrome usually share certain physical characteristics, but more importantly each child inherits his or her own family's looks and traits. Although all children with Down's syndrome will have learning difficulties, their abilities vary widely.

There are many reasons why children with Down's syndrome should be given the opportunity to attend their local school. Increasing amounts of research have been published about the capabilities of children with Down's syndrome and their potential to be successfully included in school. Our experience shows that inclusion does not lead to discrimination and brings both academic and social benefits. Children with Down's syndrome have opportunities to develop relationships with other children from their own community who also provide models for normal and age appropriate behaviour.

Successful inclusion is a key step towards preparing children with Down's syndrome to become contributing members of the community, and this benefits society. Other children in the school gain an understanding about disability and tolerance, and they learn how to care for and support children with special needs. The most important ingredient towards successful inclusion is the will of everyone involved to make it a success.

CAROL BOYS
Chief Executive, Down's Syndrome Association
http://www.ds-int.org/home

Find out more about Down's syndrome online:
UK   www.downs-syndrome.org.uk
USA   www.ndss.org   www.ndsccenter.org
Canada   www.cdss.ca
Australia   www.dsansw.org.au   www.dsav.asn.au   www.dsaq.org.au
www.actdsa.asn.au   www.downsyndrometasmania.org.au   www.dsawa.asn.au
www.downssa.asn.au   email: dsant@octa4.net.au
New Zealand   www.nzdsa.org.nz

More books by Maria de Fatima Campos published by Frances Lincoln Children's Books

B is for Brazil

In this vivid portrait of South America's largest country, Maria de Fatima Campos explores her exciting and colourful homeland in words and pictures. She illustrates the contrasts between city and rainforest, different customs and peoples, and the vibrant world of Brazilian children – at home, at school, fishing on the river and painting in the open air.

Cássio's Day: From Dawn to Dusk in a Brazilian Village

With this beautifully photographed book, young readers can find out all about Brazil as they compare and contrast Cássio's day with their own.

Victoria Goes to Brazil

Arriving in Sao Paulo, Victoria travels to Ilha Bella to meet Mum's best friend, joins a saint's procession in Paranagua, eats delicious food and visits Itu, where everything is BIG. Wherever she goes, she meets great-grandparents, aunts and uncles, cousins and friends, and leaves with wonderful memories of her big Brazilian family.

Frances Lincoln titles are available from all good bookshops.
You can also buy books and find out more about your favourite titles, authors and illustrators on our website: www.franceslincoln.com